I0817135

United Kingdom

Kaitlyn Duling

childsworld.com

Published by The Child's World®
800-599-READ • childsworld.com

Photography Credits
ID 155708789 © Sven Hansche/Dreamstime.com, cover, 1; ID 9462433 © Elaine Taylor/Dreamstime .com, cover, 1 (inset); Daniel Levin Bennett/ Shutterstock.com, 6; Sergii Figurnyi/Shutterstock .com, 7; Jaromir Chalabala/Shutterstock.com, 8 (squirrel); Graham Taylor/Shutterstock.com, 8 (red fox); Raphael Ruz/Shutterstock.com, 8 (seal); Vaclav Matous/Shutterstock.com, 8 (red deer); Melanie Hobson/Shutterstock.com, 9; tanya _tatyana/Shutterstock.com, 10; Leonid Andronov/ Shutterstock.com, 11; Farion_O/Shutterstock.com, 12; Ink Drop/Shutterstock.com, 13; Unknown/ Heritage Art/Heritage Images AiWire/Newscom, 14; Pete Hancock/Shutterstock.com, 15; Sven Hansche/Shutterstock.com, 16, 26; David Crosbie/ Shutterstock.com, 17; Dutch_Photos/Shutterstock .com, 18; Elena Rostunova/Shutterstock.com, 19; Andriy Blokhin/Shutterstock.com, 20; Leonid Andronov/Shutterstock.com, 21; Alena Veasey/ Shutterstock.com, 22; Galdric PS/Shutterstock.com, 23; Wirestock Creators/Shutterstock.com, 24; 1000 Words/Shutterstock.com, 25; Melanie Hobson/ Shutterstock.com, 27; Tom Korcak/Shutterstock .com, 28; Debby Wong/Shutterstock.com, 29; P Maxwell Photography/Shutterstock.com, 30

ISBN Information
9781503875999 (Reinforced Library Binding)
9781503876378 (Portable Document Format)
9781503876996 (Online Multi-user eBook)
9781503877610 (Electronic Publication)

LCCN
2025938639

Printed in the United States of America

About the Author

Kaitlyn Duling believes in the power of words to change hearts, minds, and actions. An avid reader and writer who grew up in Illinois, Kaitlyn loves to learn about countries around the world. She knows that knowledge is the key to a bright future, and wants to ensure that all children and families have access to high-quality information. Kaitlyn has written over one hundred books for kids and teens!

Cover: The Tower Bridge is a famous landmark in London, England. The bridge, which crosses the Thames River, was completed in 1894.

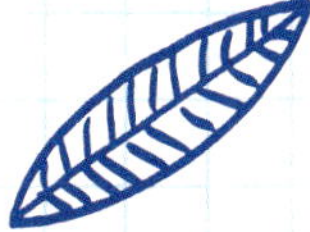

Table of Contents

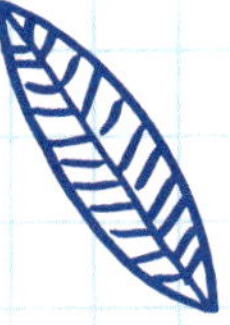

Chapter One

Where Is the United Kingdom?

Imagine that you could float high up in the air. If you look down at the Earth, you would notice that the world has many land areas that are surrounded by water. These land areas are called **continents**. Many of these continents are made up of several different countries.

The United Kingdom (UK) is an **island** country on the continent of Europe. It is made up of smaller islands. It has rugged mountains, rolling hills, and windy coastlines.

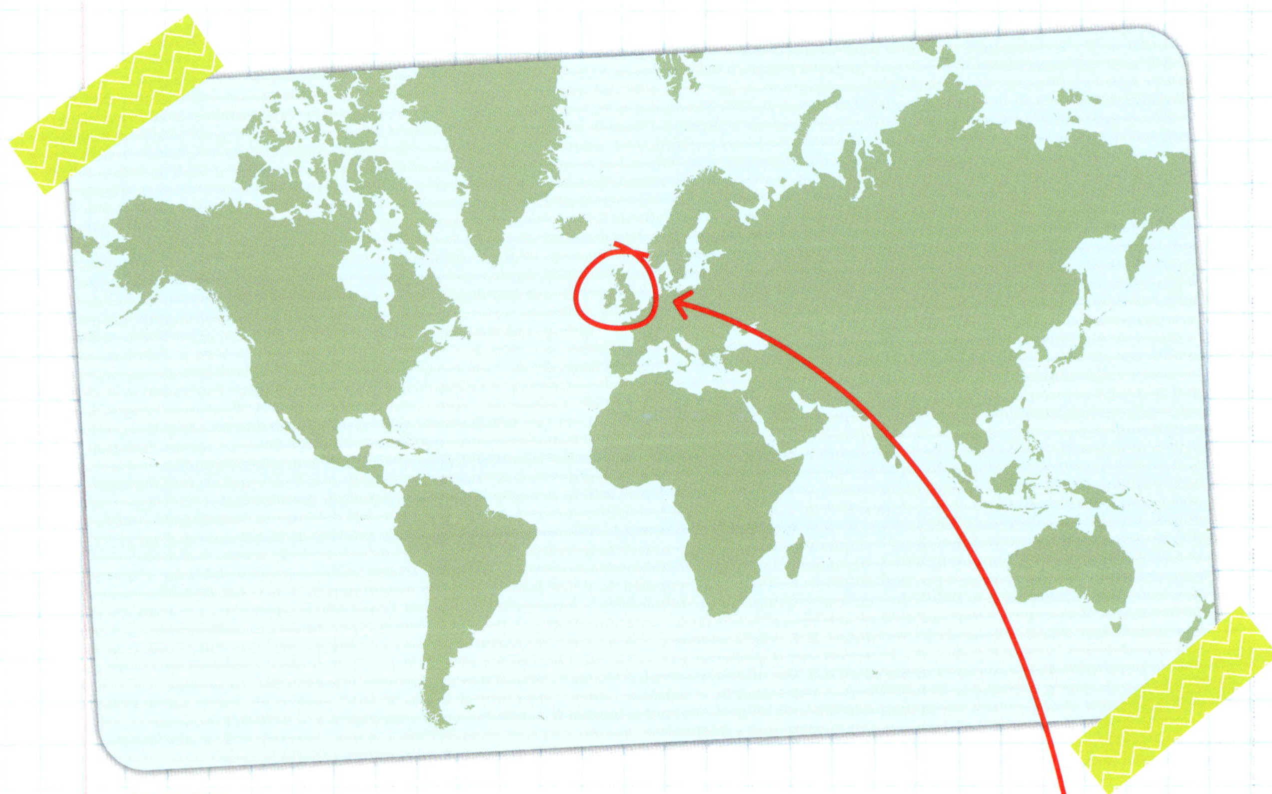

This is a flat map of the Earth. The United Kingdom is inside the red circle.

Did You Know?
The United Kingdom is one country. It is made up of four other countries: England, Scotland, Wales, and Northern Ireland.

You will need to take an airplane to get to the United Kingdom.

Chapter Two

The Land

The United Kingdom's largest island is Great Britain. It has rolling hills and flat **plains**. Great Britain is home to England, Scotland, and Wales. Scotland and Wales have mountains. The highest mountain in the UK is called Ben Nevis.

Ben Nevis is located in the Scottish Highlands. It's 4,413 feet (1,345 m) tall.

Loch Ness is known for claimed sightings of the Loch Ness Monster.

The United Kingdom has many rivers and lakes. The two largest are Lough Neagh in Northern Ireland and Loch Ness in Scotland. Lough Neagh covers more than 147 square miles (380 square kilometers)!

Did You Know?
In Scotland, lakes are called "loughs" or "lochs." Both are pronounced "LOK."

Chapter Three

Plants and Animals

The United Kingdom is home to several types of animals. Foxes, badgers, squirrels, deer, and bats can all be found there. Seals, dolphins, whales, and sharks live in the nearby waters. Visitors can see many of these animals at the Whipsnade Zoo. It is the largest zoo in the UK.

Red fox

Seal

Red deer

Squirrel

English oak trees can live for hundreds of years.

The UK is famous for its English gardens. They are filled with flowers, hedges, and trees. The English oak is one of the United Kingdom's national **emblems**. It is a large tree with bright green leaves.

Chapter Four

Long Ago

The first people in the United Kingdom were the **ancestors** of modern humans. The land was icy. The UK was connected to Northern Europe by land. When the weather heated up, hunters traveled to the UK. They followed herds of reindeer and horses. People have been moving here ever since.

Stonehenge is a famous **megalith** in England. It was built about 5,000 years ago by ancient people.

Conwy is a historic town in Wales. The castle and stone walls were built in the 1200s.

The United Kingdom used to be many separate kingdoms. Then, in the 1500s, Wales and England joined together. Scotland joined with them in 1707. Ireland joined in 1800. In 1922, the Republic of Ireland became independent. Six counties known as Northern Ireland remained part of the United Kingdom.

Did You Know?
The official name of the United Kingdom is the United Kingdom of Great Britain and Northern Ireland.

Chapter Five

The United Kingdom Today

In 1974, the United Kingdom joined the European Union (EU). The EU is a group of countries that work together. They **trade** with each other and make rules together. They try to bring peace to the region. Some countries in the EU even share the same money. It's called the euro.

The euro is used in 20 countries, but not in the UK. The money used in the UK is the British pound.

Supporters of Brexit attend a rally in 2019.

In 2016, people in the United Kingdom voted to leave the European Union. Around 52 percent of voters agreed to withdraw. So, in 2020, the United Kingdom became the first country to leave the European Union. The country's exit from the EU was called "Brexit."

Did You Know?
Brexit is a combination of the words *Britain* and *exit*. Brexit affected the United Kingdom in both good and bad ways.

Chapter Six

The People

Did You Know? The UK has been ruled by kings and queens for more than 1,200 years.

The United Kingdom once controlled many parts of the world. In the 1800s, the UK had **colonies** in North America, Asia, Africa, and more. Together, they made up the British Empire. About 23 percent of people around the globe were part of the empire. Over time, the empire shrank.

Fort Saint George was the first English fort in India. The British Empire was among the largest and most powerful in world history.

King Charles III, pictured with Queen Camilla, is the head of the British Commonwealth.

Today, many people around the world still practice **customs** from the UK. There are 56 countries in the British **Commonwealth**. Most used to be part of the British Empire. They support each other and make rules together. The king or queen of the United Kingdom leads the Commonwealth.

Chapter Seven

City Life and Country Life

The United Kingdom has many large cities. They have tall buildings and busy streets. Some cities have sports **stadiums** and old churches. In the cities, people live in flats (apartments) or houses. They travel by car, bus, or train.

London is the capital of both England and the United Kingdom.

The English countryside has traditional villages surrounded by farmland, forests, and coastal areas.

Some people in the United Kingdom live in the countryside. There are farms and small villages. Green fields are dotted with farm animals. You can even see old castles! Visitors can look inside some of them. Others are still homes.

Chapter Eight

Schools and Language

In the United Kingdom, children enter primary school at age five. At age eleven, they enter secondary school. Most students graduate when they are sixteen or eighteen. After that, they can go on to university.

The University of Cambridge in England was founded in 1209.

Some people say school uniforms help students get along better. Others say that uniforms don't allow students to express themselves through clothing.

English is taught to all students in the United Kingdom. French and Spanish are popular subjects, too. Students in Wales learn Welsh. Some students in Northern Ireland learn Irish. Some students in Scotland learn Scottish Gaelic.

Did You Know?
Most students in the United Kingdom wear school uniforms.

Chapter Nine

Work

Workers in the UK do many types of jobs. City people work at banks, hospitals, and businesses. There are also jobs in factories, schools, and restaurants. Some people work in **tourism**. They might give tours or work in a hotel.

A tour bus in London takes visitors to historic places throughout the city, including Westminster Abbey, the most famous church in the UK.

Farming and livestock are important industries in Northern Ireland.

There are small and large farms in the countryside. Farmers grow wheat, barley, potatoes, and more. Some raise cattle and sheep. Lavender farms sell sweet-smelling flowers. Tourists like to visit these farms, too.

Did You Know?
People who live in the United Kingdom are called British, or Brits.

Chapter Ten

Food

The United Kingdom is known for many delicious foods. Sunday roast and fried fish-and-chips are two of the most popular. Hot tea is a favorite drink of people in the UK.

In the United Kingdom, breakfast is a big deal. A full English breakfast includes bacon, eggs, baked beans, tomatoes, and more. It is eaten with toast. Sometimes breakfast includes blood sausage, which is made with animal blood.

The fish in fish-and-chips is usually a whitefish such as cod or haddock.

Did You Know?
The national dish of England is chicken tikka masala. It comes from India.

If you have a full English breakfast in Wales, it's called the full Welsh.

Chapter Eleven

Pastimes

There are so many ways to have fun in the United Kingdom! Football (known as soccer in the United States), rugby, and cricket are popular sports. They all started in England and are played throughout the UK. Cricket is a team sport. One team hits a ball with a bat. The other team tries to stop them. Rugby is a team sport with lots of tackling.

Rugby players score points by carrying, passing, or kicking a ball into a goal.

Large crowds attend the cheese rolling event in England every year!

Each spring, people in the UK take part in cheese rolling. A wheel of cheese is rolled down a steep hill. Hundreds of people run down the hill, chasing the cheese. The people tumble and fall down the hill. Whoever catches the cheese, wins!

Chapter Twelve

Holidays

Several holidays are celebrated in the United Kingdom. National holidays are called bank holidays. On these days, most businesses are closed. Students do not go to school. People celebrate!

People in the United Kingdom celebrate Christmas just like people in the United States.

People celebrate Bonfire Night every year on November 5.

Boxing Day is on December 26. On Boxing Day, people have parties and spend time with friends. Sometimes they play sports. Bonfire Night is November 5. On that night, people light fireworks and build fires. They're celebrating the capture of a group of people who were planning to attack the English government in 1605.

Fast Facts About the United Kingdom

Area: 94,060 square miles (243,610 square kilometers)—about a third of the size of Texas

Population: About 68,459,055 people

Capital City: London

Other Important Cities: Birmingham, Glasgow, Liverpool, Manchester

Money: Pound sterling; one pound is divided into 100 pence

National Flag: White, red, and blue. The Union Flag or Union Jack combines the Cross of St. George (England), the Cross of St. Andrew (Scotland), and the Cross of St. Patrick (Ireland).

National Holiday: The United Kingdom has no official national holiday.

National Languages: The United Kingdom does not have an official language. English is the most widely spoken language.

Head of Government: The prime minister of the United Kingdom

Head of State: The king or queen of the United Kingdom

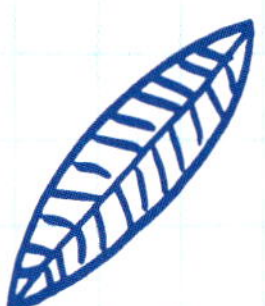

National Song: In 1745, after a battle, "God Save the King" was performed after a play. Since then, it has become a custom to greet the king or queen with the song. When a queen rules, it's changed to "God Save the Queen." The words are the same as those sung in 1745:

God save our gracious King,
Long live our noble King,
God save the King!
Send him victorious,
Happy and Glorious,
Long to reign over us;
God save the King!

Thy choicest gifts in store
On him be pleased to pour;
Long may he reign;
May he defend our laws,
And ever give us cause
To sing with heart and voice,
God save the King!

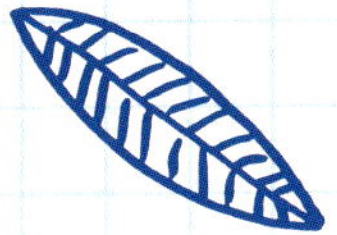
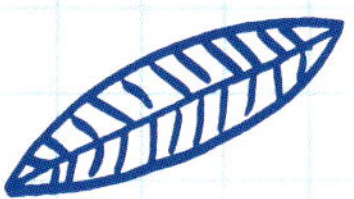

Famous People:

Julie Andrews: actor, singer

Jane Austen: author

David Beckham: former professional soccer player

Lord Byron: poet

Winston Churchill: statesman, prime minister

Charles Darwin: naturalist who developed the theory of evolution

Mo Farah: Olympic distance runner

Lewis Hamilton: Formula One race car driver

David Hockney: artist

Elton John: singer-songwriter, pianist

Florence Nightingale: founder of modern nursing

Emmeline Pankhurst: activist, suffragist

Gordon Ramsay: celebrity chef, restaurateur

Margaret Thatcher: first female prime minister of the UK

Scottish Folklore:

The Legend of Nessie
The Loch Ness Monster is a mythical creature said to live in Loch Ness, a deep lake in the Scottish Highlands. Stories about the Loch Ness Monster, nicknamed "Nessie," date back more than 1,500 years. Nessie is described as a massive creature with a long neck and humps. Sightings of Nessie have been reported over the years, but scientists can't confirm its existence.

David Beckham

Make British Shortbread

1 cup butter, softened
½ cup sugar, plus 1 teaspoon
2½ cups all-purpose flour

1. Preheat oven to 300 degrees F (149 degrees C).*
2. Cream the butter and sugar together until the mixture is smooth.
3. Add the flour. Mix with a wooden spoon or your hands. Mix until texture is like clay.
4. Press the dough into an ungreased 9 x 13 inch pan. Prick the dough with a fork, and sprinkle with sugar.
5. Place pan into the fridge to chill for 10 to 20 minutes.
6. Bake for 30 minutes, until the shortbread is very lightly browned.
7. Let stand for 5 minutes. Cut into squares while warm.
8. Let cool in pan. Enjoy your British shortbread!

*Ask a grown-up for help operating the oven.

Glossary

ancestors (AN-sess-turz) Ancestors are people who were part of a family many years ago. The first people in the United Kingdom were the ancestors of modern humans.

colonies (KOL-uh-neez) Colonies are lands with ties to a mother country. The UK once had colonies throughout the world.

commonwealth (KAH-muhn-welth) A commonwealth is a nation or state that is governed by the people who live there.

continents (KON-tih-nents) Earth is divided up into land areas called continents. The United Kingdom is an island country on the continent of Europe.

customs (KUHS-tumz) Customs are traditions in a culture or society.

emblems (EM-bluhms) An emblem is a symbol or sign that represents something. The English oak tree is an emblem of the United Kingdom.

island (EYE-luhnd) An island is a piece of land that's completely surrounded by water. The UK is made up of islands.

megalith (MEG-uh-lith) A megalith is a very large stone used to build a structure or monument. England's Stonehenge is a famous megalith.

plains (PLAYNZ) Plains are stretches of fairly flat land. Great Britain has rolling hills and flat plains.

stadiums (STAY-dee-uhmz) Stadiums are large structures where sports events and concerts are held.

tourism (TOOR-ihz-uhm) Tourism is traveling for pleasure or the business of serving and working in the traveling industry.

trade (TRAYD) Trade is the business of buying and selling goods. Countries throughout the world trade goods and services.

For More Information

READ IT

Malaspina, Ann, and Mary Manning (illustrator). *Jack and the Beanstalk: An English Folktale*. Parker, CO: The Child's World, 2025.

Waldendorf, Kurt. *Soccer Around the Globe*. Parker, CO: The Child's World, 2025.

Walker, Tracy Sue. *Spotlight on the United Kingdom*. Minneapolis, MN: Lerner, 2024.

Williams, Imogen Russell, and Louise Lockhart (illustrator). *The Big Book of the UK*. London, UK: Ladybird Books, 2019.

LOOK IT UP

Visit our website for lots of links about the United Kingdom:
childsworld.com/links

Note to Parents, Caregivers, Teachers, and Librarians: We routinely verify our web links to make sure they are safe, active sites—so encourage your readers to check them out!

Index